GREAT EXPLORATIONS

Vasco Nuñez de Balboa

Explorer of the Pacific

Steven Otfinoski

BENCHMARK BOOKS

MARSHALL CAVENDISH
NEW YORK

With special thanks to Serinity Young, Ph.D., American Museum of Natural History, for her careful reading of this manuscript.

Benchmark Books
99 White Plains Road
Tarrytown, NY 10591-9001
www.marshallcavendish.com

Library of Congress Cataloging-in-Publication Data
Otfinoski, Steven.
Vasco Nunez de Balboa : explorer of the Pacific / by Steven Otfinoski.

p. cm. — (Great explorations)
Summary: Describes the life of Vasco Nunez de Balboa, the Spanish explorer who was the first European to see the Pacific Ocean and who conceived the idea of a canal connecting the Atlantic and Pacific.
Includes bibliographical references and index.
ISBN 0-7614-1609-9
1. Balboa, Vasco Nunez de, 1475-1519—Juvenile literature. 2. Explorers—America—Biography—Juvenile literature. 3. Explorers—Spain—Biography—Juvenile literature. 4. America—Discovery and exploration—Spanish—Juvenile literature. 5. Pacific Ocean—Discovery and exploration—Spanish—Juvenile literature. [1. Balboa, Vasco Nunez de, 1475-1519. 2. Explorers. 3. America—Discovery and exploration—Spanish.] I. Title. II. Series.

E125.B2O84 2004
972.8'02'092—dc22
2003014927

Photo research by Candlepants Incorporated

Cover photo: Corbis / Colin Anderson
Cover inset: The Image Works

The photographs in this book are used by permission and through the courtesy of: *The Image Works*: 21; Venturian cover, 9; ANA, 32, 36, 50, 56, 64. *The Art Archive:* Real Monasterio del Escorial Spain/Dagli Orti, 7; Monastery of the Rabida, Palos, Spain/Dagli Orti, 11; Naval Museum Genoa/Dagli Orti, 14; Eileen Tweedy, 16; Museo del Prado Madrid/Dagli Orti, 30; Album/Joseph Martin, 60; Art Archive, 67; Archivo de Indios Seville/Album/Joseph Martin, 68. *North Wind Picture Archive:* 15, 22, 25, 37, 43, 49, 57, 61, 69. *Bridgeman Art Library:* Museo del Oror, Bogota, Colombia, 28; Library of Congress, Washington, D.C., USA, 40; Private Collection/The Stapleton Collection, 52. *Getty:* Hulton Archive, 38, 71. *Corbis:* 70.

Printed in China
1 3 5 6 4 2

Contents

foreword

The conquistadors were a bold breed of Spanish soldiers of fortune. They were the first men to explore and colonize the Americas. Most of them were sons of poor noblemen who triumphed over tremendous odds to achieve greatness.

Vasco Nuñez de Balboa was the first important conquistador. Balboa's tale of rags to riches is one of the most dramatic. While later conquistadors discovered great civilizations and empires, Balboa discovered something perhaps even greater: he was the first European to lay claim to an ocean. He also established the first permanent settlement on the mainland of the Americas.

Balboa was not only one of the first conquistadors. He was, in many ways, the best of them. He was a strong and courageous leader who treated his men and the native peoples he encountered with respect. If those men who followed in his footsteps were as well intended, the story of the Spanish empire in the New World might have turned out very differently.

But unlike books and movies, real life does not always turn out the way we would like it to. In the end, it was not poison arrows, hostile Indians, or jungle fever that brought down Balboa but the jealousy and greed of his own kind.

This is his story.

O N E

A Daring Youth

The year 1492 is important in world history for two reasons. Nearly everyone knows the first reason—Christopher Columbus discovered America. But the second reason is equally important to the great period of exploration begun by Columbus. It was in that year that the Spanish finally drove the Moors, Muslim invaders who came from North Africa, from their land.

The Moors had been in Spain for 700 years and in control of the country for much of that time. By 1492, after centuries of warfare, they remained in only one province of Spain—Granada. Their removal from their last stronghold meant Spain was finally a free and independent country.

But this great triumph was something of a disappointment for a young generation of Spanish gentlemen. They had been trained for warfare from a very young age. A soldier's life was the best career choice

o cauleiro estairo a missa o uiro na batalla lidar mui feramte

el conde ĩ o caualeiro tʒodolos crischãos loarõ muito dŝ · d̃

This illustration from a thirteenth-century manuscript depicts one of the many battles fought between Spaniards and Moors for control of Spanish territory.

for these sons of Spain. Glory in battle was their ultimate dream. With the Moors gone, that dream vanished.

However, the New World opened by Columbus provided a new path to glory. In the Americas there were untold adventures to be had, land to be taken, and riches to be discovered—gold, silver, and pearls. This was a dream even greater than the one it replaced.

One of these ambitious young men was Vasco Nuñez de Balboa, born in Jerez de los Caballeros, a small town near the Portuguese border. Balboa was about seventeen when Columbus made his first voyage to the New World. The young Spaniard was everything a future conquistador should be—intelligent, courageous, bold, and well trained in the art of swordsmanship. The only thing that the red-haired Balboa lacked was wealth. His family, although an old and noble one, had little money. Balboa's father, Don Nuño Arias de Balboa, was that saddest of Spaniards: an impoverished nobleman.

Not much is known of Balboa's early life in Spain. It is not even certain when he was born, although most historians place his birth year about 1475. It is known that he was the third of four boys and that his mother was a lady of Badajoz in southwestern Spain. It is also known that at a certain age he was sent to Moguer, a port on Spain's southwestern coast, to serve in the household of the rich governor, Don Pedro Puertocarrero. There, he worked as a page and later, it is believed, a fencing master.

At the docks of Moguer, Balboa and other young men listened intently to the stories told by sailors recently arrived from the New World. Some had sailed with Columbus on one of his voyages. The stories they told of great wealth and mysterious lands fired Balboa's imagination and his yearning for adventure. But nothing in life would come easy for Balboa. He may have been twenty-six before he had an opportunity to sail to the New World.

A Daring Youth

In 1500, King Ferdinand and Queen Isabella of Spain granted Don Rodrigo de Bastidas, a wealthy official, a license to sail and explore the northern coast of what is today South America. It was not Bastidas's ability as a navigator or explorer that won him this honor, but his wealth. He bought and outfitted two ships for his adventure. As was the custom, he agreed to give Ferdinand and Isabella a quarter of any riches he found. The rest he could keep for himself. The royal order gave him permission to sail west to look for "gold, silver, lead, tin, serpents, fishes, birds and monsters."

More specifically, Bastidas was looking for pearls. When Columbus had landed on the northern shores of South America on his third voyage in 1498, he had found it rich in pearls. Later, sailors named it *la Costa de las Perlas*, the Coast of Pearls. To assure that he would find this treasured place, Bastidas hired as his navigator Juan de la Cosa, who had sailed with Columbus.

Lustrous pearls were highly prized in fifteenth-century Spain.

COLUMBUS'S THIRD VOYAGE— THE "OTHER WORLD"

On his first voyage of 1492, Columbus is said to have "discovered" America. However, the great explorer did not officially land on the mainland of the Americas until his less celebrated third voyage in 1498.

Columbus left Spain on May 30 of that year and sailed farther south than he had on his last two previous voyages. He made his first landfall on the island of Trinidad. He next landed on the north coast of South America in present-day Venezuela. Columbus realized this was not just another island. He called it an "Other World" and "a very great continent."

Although impressed by the beautiful pearls traded by the local natives, Columbus quickly left the coast and rushed back to the islands of Hispaniola. He was governor there and concerned about the unruly Spanish settlers. In 1500, Columbus's troubles on Hispaniola led to a new governor being appointed to the island. The new governor, Francisco de Bobadilla, charged Columbus with crimes against the Spaniards and Indians on Hispaniola and had him sent back to Spain in chains.

Columbus was cleared of all charges and restored to favor by the king and queen, but he made only one more voyage to the New World. This trip largely proved to be a disaster, and Columbus returned to Spain where he died alone and forgotten in 1506. However, Columbus's discovery of the Other World had already brought Bastidas and others to its shores in search of wealth and glory.

Columbus points the way to his next landfall, Guanahani Island in the Bahamas. In all, Columbus made four voyages to the New World.

Balboa was one of a number of local young men who applied and were accepted for the voyage. His position was not as a crewmember but as an *escudero*, a fighting man, to defend the expedition from hostile natives.

In early 1501, Bastidas's ships, the *Santa Maria de Gracio* and the *San Anton*, sailed out of Moguer harbor. The adventures the explorers would experience would be greater than any they could have imagined.

T W O

To the New World

Under the steady navigational hand of Juan de la Cosa, Bastidas's small expedition soon reached the northern coasts of present-day Venezuela and Colombia. For four months, the two ships sailed along the Coast of Pearls, stopping ashore at native villages. There they traded trinkets and knives for valuable pearls the Indians harvested from local oyster beds.

Balboa, unlike many of his companions, was eager to learn about the natives' ways, neighboring tribes, and the lay of the land. In this pursuit, he found a ready teacher in Cosa, who had already been to many of these places with Columbus several years earlier. The information Balboa gathered would prove invaluable years later.

By October 1501, the expedition reached the Gulf of Urabá, a bay that cuts into present-day northwestern Colombia. From there, the Spaniards sailed west into eastern Panama where the friendly native

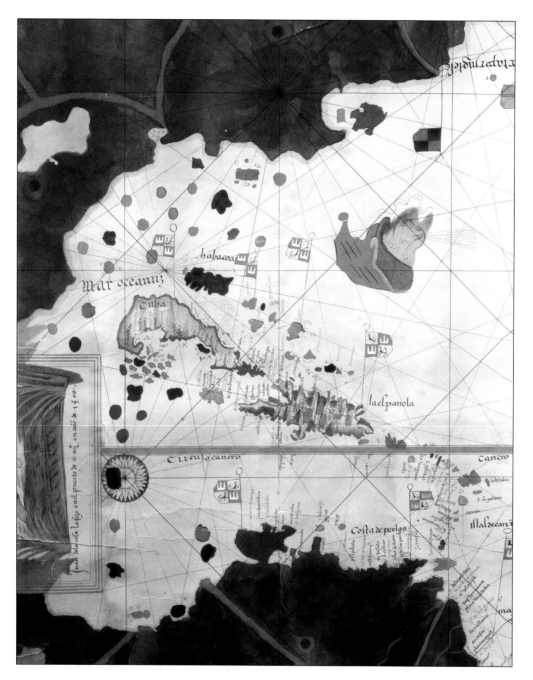

This world map, highlighting the islands of Cuba and Hispaniola, shows Juan de la Cosa to have been as skilled a mapmaker as he was a navigator.

The caravel was a sturdy, three-masted, square-rigged sailing ship favored for its lightness and speed, first by the Portuguese and then the Spanish in their voyages of exploration.

residents eagerly traded their pearls and gold to the newcomers. Bastidas kept all the pearls in three iron chests.

Months passed, but the Spaniards' days in paradise were numbered. They were under attack by a subtle enemy; tiny wormlike creatures called broma that were quietly eating away at the boards of their ships. Cosa knew the ships would soon sink, stranding them in a land that they might never be able to leave.

Cosa immediately set his course for the north and the island of Jamaica in the Caribbean Sea. At Jamaica they attempted to repair the ships to make them seaworthy. Bastidas was anxious to set sail for Spain with his treasure. But the ships would never make the Atlantic crossing. The damage from the broma was too great. Cosa set course for the nearby island of Hispaniola, the home base for all Spanish expeditions. They were within sight of the island's eastern end when the ships began

HISPANIOLA—THE SPANISH ISLAND

The first permanent Spanish settlement in the New World, Hispaniola was originally called *La Isla Espanola*, or "the Spanish island." The island was already settled when Balboa arrived there in 1502, and it remained the home base for the Spanish in the Caribbean for two decades. After that, however, most Spanish settlers left the island for richer opportunities in Mexico and Peru.

By 1600 the population of Hispaniola was almost entirely made up of black slaves and descendants of slaves brought from Africa to work the coffee and sugarcane plantations. By the end of the century, French settlers had taken over the western third of the island. A slave revolt in the 1790s led to the end of French rule and the birth of the independent republic of Haiti in 1804. The eastern two-thirds of Hispaniola broke away from Haiti forty years later to become the Dominican Republic. Today, these two countries are among the poorest in the Western Hemisphere but also possess a long and rich Spanish, French, and African heritage.

Hispaniola had been a Spanish colony for more than 130 years when this map was made in 1633. Note the large, open bay on the island's western end.

to sink. The men swam for shore, taking as many of the pearls and gold ornaments as they could safely carry.

Weary and wet, the Spaniards arrived on shore only to make another dismal discovery. They were 200 miles (322 km) from Santo Domingo, the only Spanish settlement on the island. For two weeks, they marched through rain forests and swamps, trading what trinkets they had left with the native residents for food.

They no sooner arrived in Santo Domingo than the island's governor, Nicolas de Ovando, had them arrested for trading with the Indians without permission. For a month, Bastidas, Balboa, and the others sat in prison. Finally, Ovando released them. Bastidas immediately caught a ship for Spain. He was cleared of all charges there and sold his pearls for a fortune.

Many of the men on Bastidas's expedition soon followed him back to Spain. Not Balboa. He had come to the New World to stay. He was none the richer for his experience on the Coast of Pearls, but he did have a wealth of knowledge about the places he had been.

Ovando was impressed by Balboa and his knowledge of the region. He gave him a plot of land and some Indian slaves to work it for him. Having no other means of support, Balboa took the offer. But he was no farmer. While others prospered growing corn and peppers and raising pigs, Balboa could barely make a living. Soon he was borrowing money from his neighbors just to keep his farm going. These debts became a curse to him. The law said that no person could leave Hispaniola without paying all of his or her debts. While the American mainland was only about 360 miles (579 km) away from Hispaniola, it might as well have been a thousand miles. Without money to pay his debts, Balboa was trapped.

Little is known of the eight years he spent on Hispaniola. They were probably miserable years for the still youthful explorer who yearned to discover new lands. If it was any consolation to Balboa, during his years

Rodrigo Bastidas (1460-1526)

Rodrigo Bastidas returned to Spain from his first adventure in the New World a rich man. His exploration of the northern coast of South America was a valuable contribution to the age of exploration. It confirmed Columbus's opinion that this region was rich in resources and worthy of colonization.

However, more than two decades would pass before Bastidas would return to the New World. Differences with the king and his court put him outside the privileged circle of those granted commissions to explore and settle. Finally in 1525 Bastidas was allowed to lead another expedition to South America. He discovered the mouth of the Magdalena River in Colombia and founded the settlement of Santa Marta.

Bastidas opposed those colonists who wanted to exploit the natives living in the area, and in their anger they tried to kill him. In a fight with his enemies, Bastidas was wounded and fled to Hispaniola. A storm forced his ship to land in Cuba, where he died of his wounds.

on Hispaniola, new exploration came to a near standstill. No further expeditions probed the mainland, called *Terra Firme* by the Spanish. The only places for settlement were Jamaica, Cuba, and a few other islands.

Then in 1508, two well-to-do gentlemen were given permission by King Ferdinand to explore and settle the Coast of Pearls. Alonso de Ojeda was given all the territory east of the Gulf of Urabá. Diego de Nicuesa was given all the land west of the gulf. Both young men were cunning, charming, and ambitious. Ojeda had sailed with Columbus and in 1499 explored the coast of Venezuela, but Nicuesa had no experience in the New World.

Ojeda took on a partner, Martin de Enciso, who was a lawyer on Hispaniola. His task was to follow in Ojeda's wake with more supplies and men for his colony. Enciso prepared to set off from Hispaniola in late 1510. Balboa longed to join his expedition and escape the drudgery of his life. But he had two problems. One, his debtors would not let him leave. Two, Enciso knew him and did not particularly like him. Still Balboa decided he would find a way to get on Enciso's ship. He knew if he did not, he might end his days as a pig farmer.

THREE

From Stowaway to Governor

The purpose of Martin de Enciso's voyage was to bring supplies and some new settlers to Alonso de Ojeda's colony of San Sebastián on the coast of present-day Colombia. This gave Balboa an idea for how to get aboard the ship. He offered his grain to Enciso, who readily bought it. Then Balboa hid himself in one of the casks of grain and was carried into the hold of the ship the night before it sailed. Once aboard, he hid in a sail. He had not come alone; Balboa had even brought along his faithful hound Leoncico.

Once the ship was safely at sea, Balboa came out of hiding and presented himself to Enciso. The lawyer was probably furious to find the stowaway. Yet he realized that Balboa was well liked by many on board and that the crew would not be in favor of putting him off on the nearest island. Anyway, Enciso could use a skilled swordsman once they reached San Sebastián.

Balboa comes out of hiding on Enciso's ship, much to the surprise of
the crew and passengers.

This was truer that Enciso could have known at the time. Ojeda, who had reached the mainland some time before, had left a path of blood behind him. He attacked the Indians they met on shore, killing many and taking many others as slaves. He then proceeded to march inland and took over the deserted village of Turbaco. While they were looting the village of food and gold, the Indians returned and killed nearly the entire group of Spaniards. Only Ojeda and one other soldier escaped with their lives and fled to their ships. The remaining Spaniards returned to Turbaco to punish the people. Ojeda, Nicuesa, and 400 men attacked the town before dawn. By midmorning they had killed most of the Indians. Then the Spaniards sailed west into the Gulf of Urabá

Alonso de Ojeda and his men capture the Indian chief Caonabo in present-day Colombia. Their cruelty to the Indians was returned in kind.

where Balboa had traveled a decade earlier. At the mouth of the gulf they built a fort and hut, naming the small settlement San Sebastián.

Word of Ojeda's cruelties had preceded him. The local Indians picked off the soldiers one by one as they built their dwellings. They had a terrible weapon to match the firepower of the Spanish guns: arrows dipped in the juice of a poisonous herb. To be pierced by one of these arrows meant certain death for the victim; the Spanish had no antidote to the poison. Among the early casualties was Balboa's old friend, Juan de la Cosa.

The Spaniards were trapped in their fort, unable to search or hunt for food because of the danger the Indians posed. Finally Ojeda decided to sail to Hispaniola for help and supplies. He left a courageous soldier named Francisco Pizarro in charge of the settlement. The days passed slowly for those left behind, many of whom continued to be picked off by the Indians.

After fifty days, Pizarro abandoned San Sebastián with his men and set sail in their two ships for Cartagena in present-day Colombia. One ship was driven by winds and currents to Cuba, and Pizarro arrived at Cartagena with only 35 of the original 300 men left behind by Ojeda.

They arrived to meet Enciso's ship and told the terrible tale of their adventure to the newcomers. Enciso, who was as lacking in good judgment as Ojeda, insisted on going to San Sebastián and wanted Pizarro to guide him there. They arrived to find the fort and all thirty huts burned to the ground. No sooner did Enciso set his men to work rebuilding the settlement than the Indians returned with their poisonous arrows.

Enciso was uncertain what to do next. In a rare display of democratic leadership, he turned to his men for advice. The majority voted to return to the safety of Hispaniola. But Balboa had wasted the last eight years of his life on the island and had no intention of returning there. He had a better plan.

Balboa was not a gifted speaker, but he spoke with the assured voice of experience. He told the men that he had been a little farther west of the Gulf of Urabá where the Darién Indians lived. These natives were peaceful people, he told them, and more importantly, did not "put the herb on their arrows." They also had gold and pearls to trade.

The men voted to go to this more attractive region, and Enciso reluctantly agreed to let Balboa lead them there. The 200 men sailed into the gulf, landed on shore, and marched into the nearest Indian village. Contrary to what Balboa had said, the Darién Indians attacked the soldiers. The Spaniards fired on them, killing a number of them. The others fled.

At this point, Balboa did something that would never have occurred to Ojeda or Enciso. He met with the local *cacique*, or chief, Cemaco, and made peace with him. Throughout his encounters with native peoples he would follow this same pattern. If they were friendly, he would be their friend. If they fought him, he would fight back fiercely, but once the fighting stopped, he always sought to make peace with the tribe. On most occasions, this approach was met with friendship. Balboa wanted the natives as his allies and partners, not enemies to be killed and enslaved. Few other conquistadors took such an enlightened attitude.

With no immediate threat of native attack, the Spaniards set about creating a new settlement. They called it Santa Maria la Antigua del Darién, or for short, Darién. It would be the first successful European settlement on the North American mainland.

Enciso reasserted his authority in Darién. He declared that all trading with the Indians had to be authorized by him. Anyone who traded on his own was to be put to death. The men resented Enciso and the fact that he intended to keep all the gold they found for himself. Furthermore, they had little respect for a nobleman who was so unskilled in the arts of survival in this new land.

The Indians of San Sebastián used shooting tubes like this one for their poisonous arrows.

Balboa, on the other hand, had proven a fair and experienced leader. He pointed out a fact that Enciso had overlooked. Darién lay west of the boundary line of Ojeda's territory. According to the king's proclamation, it belonged to Nicuesa, who so far had not appeared to claim it.

Since Enciso could claim no power in Darién, the men elected new leaders. Balboa and Benito Palazuelos were elected joint *alcaldes*, or mayors, of Darién. Martin de Zamudio, who was elected alderman, later replaced Palazuelos as the other *alcalde*. Balboa would be the temporary governor of the entire territory until Nicuesa arrived on the scene.

Enciso had no choice but to accept this decision. But inwardly he seethed with fury towards the stowaway who had now replaced him.

FOUR
The First Conquistador

Balboa soon proved himself worthy of the trust and support of the men of Darién. He traded with the natives for gold and shared the wealth equally with all, something Enciso would have never done. He oversaw the planting of crops to improve the food supply. He explored the region beyond Darién in present-day Panama, making friends with the native peoples and adding more territory to the Spanish crown.

In November 1510, two ships entered the Gulf of Urabá. Rodrigo Enriquez de Colmenares, Diego de Nicuesa's lieutenant, was in command. Colmenares was returning to Nicuesa's colony of Veragua with supplies and new recruits.

Balboa explained that he was keeping the new settlement in Nicuesa's name and would give up his position if and when Nicuesa arrived there. Colmenares was impressed by Balboa and his leadership

The lure of treasure and golden ornaments like this one was what brought the Spaniards to Central and South America.

and gave him supplies from his ships. Then he set off to find Nicuesa with two of Balboa's men accompanying him.

It did not take Colmenares long to find Nicuesa. He and his men were stranded along the coast in a harbor they had named *Nombre de Dios*, the Name of God. Nicuesa had set out with nearly 800 men, and only about 65 were left. The others had died from fever, disease, and Indian attacks under Nicuesa's inept leadership.

But Colmenares's news of Darién raised Nicuesa's spirits. He prepared to sail for the settlement at once to claim it as his own. What exactly happened when he arrived there is unclear. News of Nicuesa's intention to punish Balboa and his men for trading with the Indians preceded his arrival. The men decided in a town meeting not to accept him as their leader. What role Balboa played in this decision is uncertain. Nicuesa may have spent several weeks at Darién as Balboa's guest, or the men of Darién may have voted not to allow him to set foot in their settlement. Whichever the case, the final outcome is clear. Nicuesa, under force, sailed away with seventeen men on March 1, 1511. Colmenares and forty-eight of his men joined Balboa's settlement. Neither Nicuesa nor any of his crew were ever heard from again. They either drowned at sea or were killed by hostile native peoples, possibly after landing on the island of Cuba.

Nicuesa was gone, but Enciso remained very much a threat to Balboa's authority. At the first opportunity, the lawyer departed on a ship for Hispaniola and then to Spain. Balboa knew that once he arrived back in Spain he would do everything he could to have Balboa replaced as governor. Wisely, Balboa sent his closest ally and partner, Zamudio, on the same ship to plead his case before the king.

Meanwhile, Balboa continued to explore his domain. He sailed to Careta, which was ruled by the powerful chief Chima. After the Indians lost the ensuing battle, Balboa made peace with Chima and they

This idealized portrait of King Ferdinand captures little of the
strength and determination that helped him make Spain
into a major European power.

Ferdinand V – Father of Modern Spain (1452–1516)

King Ferdinand V remains one of Spain's most famous monarchs and for very good reasons.

Before Ferdinand's marriage to his cousin Isabella in 1469, there was no Spain as we know it today. Instead there was a group of individual, competing kingdoms, the two largest being Castile and Aragon. Isabella ruled Castile, and Ferdinand was king of Aragon. Their marriage united these two kingdoms, establishing a new nation that would become Spain.

With their successful war against the Moors and their support of Columbus's voyages to the New World, Ferdinand and Isabella started Spain on the road to its golden age, which would last for about a century.

After Isabella's death in 1504, Ferdinand married the young Germaine de Foix, niece of Louis XII of France. It was partly a political marriage. For all the explorations of his countrymen, Ferdinand was more interested in Spain's role in Europe than in the New World. He fought a war with France in 1501 over Italy and gained both the Italian city-state of Naples and the French province of Navarre.

Yet Ferdinand closely followed the progress of his conquistadors and became close to several of them, including Juan Ponce de León, a friend of Balboa's, who is credited with discovering Florida.

Ferdinand died in 1516 and was succeeded by his grandson Charles I.

became the closest of friends. Chima even gave Balboa his beautiful, young daughter, whose name remains lost to history, as a gift. She lived in the conquistador's home as his ward, later becoming his devoted mistress. She was invaluable as a liaison to other tribes.

Balboa takes Chief Chima's daughter as a gift, cementing his relationship with the Indians in the region.

For all his success in Darién, Balboa knew that his position was a shaky one. He sincerely felt that he had done nothing wrong in expelling Nicuesa, who was rejected by his own men. But Enciso had powerful friends at court, and they could have Balboa removed from power.

To legitimatize his position as governor, Balboa believed he had to, as Columbus did, make some great discovery. He had heard from several of his Indian allies of a great sea over the mountains to the west that was as mighty as the Atlantic Ocean. Furthermore, the Indians told him about a great civilization to the south that could be reached by sailing on this ocean. Their wealth, so it was said, surpassed that of the peoples of the Coast of Pearls and the Gulf of Urabá. These people were called the Inca and lived in the land of Biru, or Peru. Balboa decided he would find this great sea and then visit the Inca.

When he returned to Darién from his adventures, Balboa found that ships had arrived from Spain with two letters. The letters contained good news and bad news. The good news was that the king had officially appointed Balboa the captain-general and interim governor of Darién. The bad news was that the king had offered the post to another man—who had declined. Balboa was concerned that his governorship might be short lived.

Balboa wasted no time in writing a detailed letter of his own to the king. In the letter, dated January 20, 1520, Balboa explained in great detail his accomplishments and his loyalty to the king. Then he described the great sea he hoped to find and the people who lived on its shores. "I have learned very great secrets from them [the Indians] and things whereby one can secure very great riches and [a] large quantity of gold, which your Royal Highness will be very much served."

Balboa then boldly asked the king for a fresh supply of weapons and food and 1,000 men from Hispaniola to accompany him on this great expedition. The letter went out on the next ship for Spain.

Months passed, and no word came from Spain. By August Balboa decided he could wait no longer for a reply. He would set off, with or without the king's permission, and hope to return a hero.

He selected 190 of the best men of Darién and 800 Indians to carry supplies and serve as guides. On September 1, 1513, with his dog Leoncico by his side, Balboa led his expedition out of Darién in search of this unknown sea.

f I V E

To the Other Sea

The narrow strip of land that separated the Atlantic from this so-called other sea is called an isthmus. Although Balboa did not know it at the time, it was less than 50 miles (80 km) wide. But the distance was deceptive. The land route cut through some of the thickest rain forests in Central and South America.

Balboa's first stop was at the village of his good friend Chima. The party rested there for two days, while Balboa reviewed the journey with Chima and made final preparations. They left the morning of September 3 with Indian guides provided by the chief. Balboa was the first Spanish explorer to use native guides. Later conquistadors followed his example.

The first leg of their journey took them through a swampy region called Balsas. Besides swamps, there were rivers and streams to cross. Many times the men stripped their armor and most of their clothing, placed it on their shields, and carried it on top of their heads. After four

Balboa's march across the isthmus of Panama was relatively short but
was filled with every kind of hardship and danger.

An Indian points Balboa in the direction of the Pacific. Note the explorer's faithful dog Leoncico on the right.

torturous days, they reached the more passable lowlands. They entered a rain forest next, where the trees and plant life were so thick Balboa and his men could not see the sky. The forest continued part way up the mountainside, at which point they reached the Indian village of Ponca.

This illustration captures the drama and historical significance of Balboa's first sight of the Pacific Ocean.

Balboa had been there before, and the friendly villagers exchanged gifts with the Spaniards. The chief provided Balboa with fresh guides and porters, and the conquistador sent Chima's men back to their village.

On September 20, they left the village and began the difficult ascent of the mountains. Along the way they encountered deep, wide streams

JOHN KEATS'S MISTAKE

In his poem "On First Looking into Chapman's Homer," written in 1816, English poet John Keats immortalized Balboa's discovery of the Pacific. Unfortunately, he gave credit to the wrong explorer.

The fourteen-line sonnet ends with these stirring lines:

> . . . like stout Cortez when with eagle eyes
> He star'd at the Pacific—and all his men
> Look'd at each other with a wild surmise—
> Silent, upon a peak in Darien.

Hernando Cortéz conquered the Aztec empire in Mexico eight years *after* Balboa sighted the Pacific.

Keats, not quite twenty-one, wrote the poem after staying up all night with a friend reading George Chapman's translation of Homer's Greek epic *The Odyssey*. It is generally considered one of his first truly great poems, despite the historical error it contains.

and beautiful but treacherous waterfalls. Four days later, their goal almost in sight, they had their first and only encounter with hostile Indians. One thousand Quarequa warriors led by their chief Torecha attacked them with full force. Fierce as they were, the Indians were no match for Spanish muskets and steel. As many as 600 Quarequa died in the battle. Balboa did not lose a single man, although some were wounded. The wounded were left at a friendly village, and Balboa made the final push with seventy men.

Early the following morning, September 25, an Indian guide pointed to a mountain peak not far away and told Balboa that a man could see the great sea from the top. The leader told his men to break

Under Balboa's supervision, local Indians secure a wooden cross to mark the site of his great discovery.

camp. He then made the final climb, accompanied only by his dog Leoncico. Balboa wanted to savor the moment of triumph alone. For two hours he climbed. He finally reached the peak, exhausted but happy, at 10 A.M.

In one of the great moments in the history of exploration, the thirty-eight-year-old Balboa gazed in awe at the sparkling blue waters of the Pacific Ocean. He fell to his knees and prayed. Balboa was the first European to see this mighty ocean, at least from its eastern shore.

A few moments later, Balboa gestured to his men to follow him. They reached his side excitedly crying, "The sea! The sea!" Andres de Valdarrabano, a priest and the recorder of the expedition, led them in prayer. He wrote in his journal what happened next:

> . . . the captain caused a fine tree to be felled, of which was made a tall cross which was planted and fixed on that same place and high hill from where that austral [southern] sea was first seen . . . he also commanded that the names of all the men who were there with him should be written down so that the memory should remain of him and of them, because they were the first Christians who saw that sea . . .

SIX

Discoverer of the Pacific

Having seen the great sea from a distance, Balboa was anxious to get a closer look at it. The party began down the western side of the mountains. But just before they reached the shore, they came up against one more obstacle. A tribe of Indians, led by their chief Chapes, refused to let the Spaniards pass. When the intruders fired their muskets, however, the Indians fled.

Instead of pushing on down to the ocean, Balboa paused long enough to coax the Indians back and offer them his friendship. Like so many chiefs before him, Chapes accepted Balboa's friendship and invited him and his men to rest in his village. Balboa, who was exhausted, accepted his hospitality and spent two days among the Indians.

On the third day, September 29, he left the village with twenty-six men; the others, too weak to travel, remained as Chapes's guests.

Another dramatic moment is illustrated as Balboa wades into the
Gulf of San Miguel and claims the Pacific Ocean and
all lands bordering it for Spain.

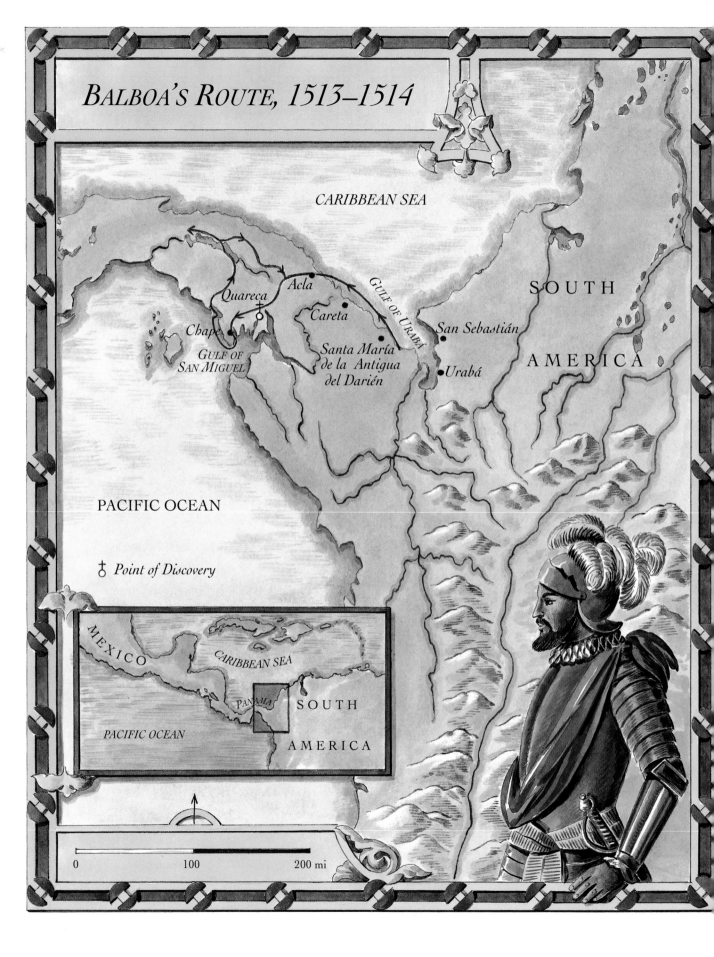

BALBOA'S ROUTE, 1513–1514

CARIBBEAN SEA

SOUTH

Acla

Quareca

Careta

GULF OF URABÁ

San Sebastián

Chape

AMERICA

GULF OF
SAN MIGUEL

Santa María
de la Antigua
del Darién

Urabá

PACIFIC OCEAN

☩ Point of Discovery

MEXICO

CARIBBEAN SEA

PANAMA

SOUTH

PACIFIC OCEAN

AMERICA

0   100   200 mi

The water's shore lay only a mile below the village. When they reached it, Balboa waded into the warm waters in full armor until it reached his knees. Then he drew his sword with one hand, brandishing the flag of Spain in the other.

In a carefully prepared speech, he declared the ocean and all lands that surrounded it the property of the king "now and for all time so long as the world shall last until the final universal judgment of all mortals." Balboa named the body of water the South Sea and the inlet he waded in the Gulf of San Miguel because September 29 was Saint Michael's (Miguel's) Day.

Next he had his men take an oath of allegiance to Spain and then returned to shore to rest in the shade of a tree with the faithful Leoncico. Meanwhile, the men tasted the salty water of the Pacific, reassuring themselves that it was an ocean like the Atlantic, which at that time was called the North Sea. Some men carved their initials in nearby tree trunks to mark the occasion.

Balboa and his party later returned to Chapes's village to rest some more. Chapes enjoyed Balboa's company and told him about a string of islands off shore so rich in pearls that they were called the Pearl Islands.

Balboa insisted on seeing the islands and Chapes agreed to take him there, although it was autumn and the stormy season. Some sixty Spaniards climbed into nine canoes, each paddled by a team of Indians. They were about 4 miles (6.4 km) from shore when a rainstorm struck. They made for the nearest shelter, a tiny island. There the Spaniards and their Indian guides spent an unpleasant night waist-deep in water. In the morning they returned to the shore, only to walk into the village of a rival tribe, led by the warrior chief Tumaco. A fight broke out. No sooner was it over than Balboa extended the hand of friendship to Tumaco. The chief became Balboa's newest ally and added to the Spaniard's treasure with basketfuls of pearls as well as gold.

THE MIGHTY PACIFIC — BALBOA'S SOUTH SEA

Balboa recognized the sea he discovered was an important one, but he could not know just how important. Today we know the Pacific Ocean is the largest and deepest body of water on Earth. Because he had traveled south across the isthmus of Panama to reach it, Balboa named it the South Sea, when, in fact, it lay west of the Atlantic Ocean.

Seven years after Balboa's discovery, Ferdinand Magellan, a Portuguese navigator sailing for Spain, entered the ocean after rounding the southern tip of South America. He renamed it the Pacific because he found its waters to be calm and peaceful. The name was deceptive, for the Pacific gives birth to some of the most powerful storms, including gigantic tidal waves and deadly typhoons.

Despite these early discoveries, the Pacific Ocean would not be fully explored for another two and a half centuries when British explorer Captain James Cook would sail across its waters.

Later Chapes told Balboa that the greatest stores of gold were to be found among the Incas of Peru. Once more Balboa listened intently to tales of the Incas, and he resolved once more to visit their land.

This expedition would have to wait, however. Balboa was anxious to return to Darién and send a full report of his discovery of the South Sea to King Ferdinand. He felt confident that his position as governor was secure. But events in Spain were shaping a very different future for the discoverer of the Pacific.

S E V E N

A New Rival

If the journey to the South Sea was difficult, the road back to Darién was even harsher. Balboa, ever the explorer, decided to take a different route, one that would allow him and his men to see more of the countryside. The party traveled through the territories of several chiefs and conquered them one after another. At the province of Tubanama, ruled by Tamaname, the Spaniards attacked the village before dawn. The Spaniards won the battle but were left exhausted and weak. The men were hungry, and Balboa was racked with fever. He halted their march and rested for four days.

They finally reached Darién after an absence of nearly five months. The expedition faced many hardships and dangers in these months, but to Balboa's credit, he had not lost a single man.

Balboa was surprised to find Darién alive with new arrivals. Four ships had recently come from Hispaniola. Among the new soldiers and

The Spaniards had to fight their way back to Darién,
as several different tribes attacked them along the way.

settlers was a man named Pedro de Arbolancha. Arbolancha called himself a trader, but, in fact, he was King Ferdinand's spy. His mission was to find out what kind of man this Vasco Nuñez de Balboa really was. Ferdinand had received contrary reports about Balboa's character from Enciso, who hated him, and Zamudio, who was his friend. Ferdinand was counting on Arbolancha to sort out the truth about the bold governor of Darién.

Everything Arbolancha heard about Balboa was positive. The men of Darién praised him for his honesty, fairness, courage, and intelligence.

Balboa's men bear the conquistador, sick with fever,
on a litter back to Darién.

Arbolancha's own judgment of the conquistador was the same. There was no evil, no guile, and no cruelty in Balboa. He was what he appeared to be—a loyal and trustworthy subject of the king. After receiving only the most favorable reports about the conquistador, Arbolancha probably revealed his true identity to Balboa.

Arbolancha was impatient to return to Spain and pass the news along to the king. But there were no available ships. The broma worms had seriously damaged those ships already in port, and they were under repair. Balboa took advantage of the delay and wrote the king a long, detailed letter of his accomplishments and gave it to Arbolancha to deliver personally.

Ferdinand was already pleased with his temporary governor in Darién. Still, the contrary reports about Balboa's character troubled him. Enciso had told him that Balboa intended to set himself up as dictator of Darién. While he waited for Arbolancha's return, Ferdinand appointed a new governor of Darién under whom Balboa would work. Relying heavily on the advice of the powerful Bishop Juan Rodriguez de Fonseca, an esteemed cleric, he chose Pedro Arias de Ávila (known as Pedrarias Dávila or merely Pedrarias), a middle-aged soldier and nobleman.

In retrospect, the king could not have made a worse choice. Pedrarias was in many ways the direct opposite of Balboa. He was narrow minded, scheming, and often cruel. Even before he left Spain, Pedrarias was determined to ruin Balboa and destroy his reputation. In light of Arbolancha's report, this probably would have been impossible. Unfortunately, Arbolancha did not arrive back in Spain until after Pedrarias's expedition had left for Darién in February 1514. The delay in the receipt of the reports would make all the difference to Balboa.

Pedrarias's expedition was one of the grandest yet to set sail for the New World. It consisted of 22 ships and some 1,500 soldiers, nobles, officials, and settlers and their wives. Pedrarias even brought his wife, Doña Isabel, and the powerful bishop Quievedo on the voyage. All the

This elegant governor's palace and formal garden on seventeenth-century Hispaniola is a far cry from Balboa's humble dwelling in Darién at the time of Pedrarias's arrival.

participants expected to find Darién to be a golden city of untold riches and greatness. The king himself had renamed it *Castilla del Oro* or "Golden Castile."

When they arrived there three months later, they were astounded to find their golden city to be a frontier settlement of thatched huts and dirt roads. But what most shocked Pedrarias was Balboa himself. He expected him to be rude, suspicious, and resentful. Instead, Balboa was a gracious host and gentleman. Although he probably was not pleased to have to turn over authority to Pedrarias, he showed nothing but respect for his successor. He even invited the new governor and his wife to stay at his house.

Pedrarias returned Balboa's hospitality by having him arrested. According to Spanish law, a new governor could have the previous governor restricted to his house for sixty days while he examined the official records and called on anyone with complaints against the official to come forward. Balboa had no problem with this situation, feeling rightly that he had nothing to hide or fear. But he did not count on Pedrarias's spite.

Pedrarias charged Balboa with the death of Nicuesa. He also brought up old charges of improper leadership laid down by Enciso, who had accompanied him to Darién. The trial dragged on for months. Meanwhile, news came from Spain that hurt Pedrarias's case. King Ferdinand sent letters that praised Balboa to the skies. " . . . I was rejoined to read letters and to learn of the things that you discovered in those regions of *Tierra Nueva de las Mar del Sur* [The New Land of the South Sea] . . ." Ferdinand wrote. "I am pleased with the way you behaved to the chiefs on that march, with kindness and forbearance . . . " In a letter dated March 1515, he named Balboa the Admiral of the Sea, a title previously given to only one person—Christopher Columbus. In addition, he made Balboa governor of the South Sea, Panama, and the island of Cuba.

Reluctantly Pedrarias suspended the trial. Balboa was a free man and ready to begin exploring again, to make new discoveries in the king's name. It now appeared Pedrarias was the one in trouble. Of the 1,500 people who were part of his expedition only a miserable few remained. The rest had been claimed by Indians, hardship, or disease. Besides this, Pedrarias, unlike Balboa, had treated the Indians cruelly, forcing them to work as slaves for the Spaniards. This led the Indians to rebel, costing the Spaniards dearly in both expense and human lives.

Balboa appeared safe from Pedrarias's schemes. Pedrarias, to make amends with his rival, even offered him his eldest daughter in marriage. Balboa seemed ready to enter a new and greater chapter of his life, but all was not as it seemed.

EIGHT

A Last Adventure

Balboa, through all his troubles with Pedrarias, still yearned to set off for the land of the Incas in Peru. But to do so, he would need seaworthy ships that could sail across the South Sea and down the South American coast. Such ships were in short supply. The broma worms continued to devastate the existing fleet, and nothing could be done to stop their destruction.

From an Indian friend Balboa had heard of a region to the north along the coast where trees grew with wood so bitter that the broma would not bore into it. These trees, Balboa believed, would be the perfect material for new ships.

The conquistador's plan was as bold as anything he had yet devised. The trees were to be cut on the east coast and then carried by Indian laborers across the mountains of the isthmus to the west coast. There, the wood would be used to build ships that could be launched

Balboa works alongside his men, felling trees to build ships he
hoped to sail south to the land of the Incas. The project
unfortunately proved to be a disaster.

Cardinal Ximenez assumed temporary control of Spain after King Ferdinand's death. He was a humane leader and defender of Indians' rights in the New World.

directly into the Gulf of San Miguel. Balboa's ultimate goal was to sail them down the coast to Peru.

It was an enormous undertaking. Large crews of Indians and soldiers, including Balboa himself, chopped down the trees and sawed them into logs and then into timbers. They dragged the timbers through the steaming rain forest to the mountains and then hauled them up the steep slopes. After resting briefly on the mountaintop, they dragged the wood down to the coast. It was backbreaking work, although the later charge that as many as 2,000 Indians died in getting the trees to the western shore of Darién is unfounded and probably started by Pedrarias.

Once work began on the ships, Balboa discovered to his horror that his friend had been wrong. The broma worms were already boring into the wood. Another man would have given up and gone back to Darién. But not Balboa. He ordered his men and the Indians to take what good wood was left from the haul and build two ships. Then he had the men chop down fresh trees and build two more ships from the timbers.

Meanwhile, back in Darién, Pedrarias was facing problems of his own. King Ferdinand died in 1516, and Cardinal Ximinez emerged as the leader of a temporary Spanish government. Ximinez was a far more humane clergyman than Bishop Fonseca was. For him, the welfare of the Indians in the New World was as important as gold and pearls. He ordered a thorough investigation of the treatment of the Indians by Spanish officials. Pedrarias, who had been cruel and merciless to the Indians in Darién, had reason to worry.

With his ships completed, Balboa set off along the coast. He hoped to at least make it to the Pearl Islands on this exploratory expedition. He was only 100 miles (161 km) from Darién when the ships ran into a pod, or group, of whales. Balboa wanted to press on, but the crew of his ships pleaded with him to turn back, fearing the whales would sink their vessels. He reluctantly agreed to do so and headed for the shore. Even if they had gotten past the whales, Balboa realized the ships were too small and fragile to reach Peru. He would need larger, sturdier ships for such a long voyage.

Balboa's last adventure was his most disappointing and costly. After a year and a half of hard work he had little to show for his efforts. When he arrived back on the western shore of Darién, he received some surprising news. Cardinal Ximinez had disapproved greatly of Pedrarias and his treatment of the Indians. He had named a new governor, Lope de Sosa, to replace him in Darién.

NINE

The final Treachery

Balboa received the news that Darién was to have a new governor with
mixed feelings. While he didn't like Pedrarias, a new governor might
be even worse. Before he made another move, he decided on a plan.
He would send five men to Darién from the western coast to deliver a
report on his progress to Pedrarias, asking for more support. One of
them, Luis Botello, was to go another route to Acla, a small outpost near
the northern coast, and Careta to find out if the new governor, Lope de
Sosa, had assumed control. If he had, Botello was to backtrack to
inform the others before reaching Darién. They would then return
immediately to Balboa. Balboa knew that a new governor would want
to approve of his explorations personally. This would take time and
slow his plans to build new ships and explore Peru. It was a delay
Balboa was eager to avoid. Wishing to futher his expedition without
interference, Balboa could always say later that he did not know that
Sosa had arrived.

Francisco Pizarro had been Balboa's lieutenant and friend, but that didn't stop him from betraying Balboa on Pedrarias's orders.

FRANCISCO PIZARRO
(C. 1475–1541)

Pizarro's early life closely paralleled that of Balboa. He was about the same age and came from an even poorer family. He never learned to read or write. Pizarro first traveled to the New World in 1502, shortly after Balboa. He too lived on Hispaniola and left in 1509 with Ojeda's ill-fated expedition.

After his betrayal of Balboa in 1519, Pizarro's star rose. Under Pedrarias's support, he became one of the wealthiest and most powerful men in Panama. He mounted an expedition to Peru in 1524, but failed to conquer the Inca empire. In 1528 Pizarro returned to Spain, where the new king Charles V gave him the authority to conquer Peru and become its Spanish governor.

He led another expedition in 1531 and within two years seized the Inca capital of Cuzco. Pizarro destroyed the Inca and their culture and set up a new capital city of Lima, where he governed with his brothers. Along the way, Pizarro made many enemies among the other Spaniards, including Diego de Almagro, who had previously been his partner. Almagro was killed during a civil war in 1538. But Pizarro continued to remain in power for only a short time. In 1541 a group of Almagro's son's supporters attacked and murdered him in his palace in Lima.

It was Pizarro, not Balboa, who would end up conquering the Inca empire of Peru and becoming one of the wealthiest of the conquistadors.

It was a good plan, but it quickly went awry. Botello was apprehended by a watchman at Acla, and Pedrarias was informed of Balboa's "plot." The other four men were arrested and held at Acla.

Pedrarias now saw an opportunity to redeem himself while getting rid of Balboa at the same time. By proving Balboa to be a traitor to Spain, he might make his own acts look less insidious. Pedrarias first had to draw Balboa to the eastern coast, but he was smart enough to know that he could not arrest Balboa in Darién. Balboa had too many friends there, and they might save him from Pedrarias's clutches. Instead, he wrote a friendly letter, asking Balboa to meet him in Acla to discuss the details of his projected expedition to Peru. Then Pedrarias sent supplies to Acla to make himself favorable in the eyes of the residents there. They would be less likely to rise up against him when he put Balboa on trial.

The messengers who brought Pedrarias's letter to Balboa warned the conquistador that the governor was trying to lure him into a trap. Balboa dismissed the warning. Perhaps he felt that he was too important and that Pedrarias would not dare to arrest him. He was so confident that he brought only a few men with him to Acla for protection.

When Balboa's small party approached Acla, his old friend Francisco Pizarro was there to meet him. Pizarro had first met Balboa on his arrival at Cartagena. He had been by his side as he founded the settlement of Darién. Pizarro was with Balboa as he crossed the isthmus and discovered the Pacific. He had been one of his most trusted lieutenants. But now Pizarro decided he had more to gain with Pedrarias than with his old leader. He coldly ordered his guard to arrest Balboa.

Balboa was charged with treason for plotting to sail to Peru and set up a dictatorship there. Charges made against him in his first trial, including the death of Nicuesa, were also brought up. Andres de Garabito, one of the five men sent to Darién earlier, testified falsely against Balboa. He harbored deep resentment against his leader, possibly over

PEDRARIAS DAVILA, THE WRATH OF GOD (1440–1531)

Pedrarias Davila seemed to live a charmed life. Not only did he escape punishment for his treatment of Balboa, but the new governor, Lope de Sosa, who arrived in Darién in May 1520, died the very night of his arrival. Pedrarias won the support of Sosa's family and was reinstated as governor.

He quickly became one of the richest and most powerful men in Spanish America. Immediately after Balboa's death, he founded a new capital, Panama, later to become Panama City. He also established the settlement that eventually became present-day Nicaragua. He remained in power in Panama for twelve years.

For the Indians of Central America and many of the Spaniards who worked under his rule, Pedrarias was known as *Furos Domini*, the Wrath of God. Even Francisco Pizarro, whose treacherous ways rivaled those of the governor, felt that wrath. Pedrarias initially helped Pizarro in his expedition to Peru and his conquest of the Inca empire. Later, however, jealous of Pizarro's growing power and achievements, Pedrarias turned against him. Pizarro and his followers succeeded in finally driving Pedrarias out of Panama in 1526. He moved to Nicaragua where he continued in power until his death in 1531 at about the age of ninety. Few mourned his passing.

his rejection by Balboa's Indian wife some time earlier. Garabito was pardoned for giving evidence against his friend.

Balboa vehemently denied all the charges, but he was not allowed to testify in his own behalf. The judge in the trial, Espinosa, had been promised new honors and powers by Pedrarias if he found Balboa guilty. The brief trial was a sham. Espinosa found Balboa and four of his six companions guilty. He hesitated to proclaim the sentence of death, believing only the courts in Spain could do that. But Pedrarias insisted and got his way. He was anxious to see the sentence carried out quickly, before word reached Darién and Balboa's supporters rose up in rebellion.

Balboa's trial, conviction, and execution at Acla in January 1519 were a gross miscarriage of justice.

Sometime between January 10 and 21 in 1519 (some historians believe it was January 12, others January 15), Balboa and his four co-defendants were led in chains into Acla's public square. One account describes how Balboa once more before the execution block declared his innocence. It then continues:

> *His declaration availed him not at all. And thus, he having confessed and partaken of communion and put his soul in order as well as the time and the event allowed, they cut off his head.*

The other four followed him to the block. Balboa's body was buried on the mountainside. His head was mounted on a pole where it remained for several days. It was another dark day in the history of the New World.

Afterword

In many ways, Vasco Nuñez de Balboa was a model explorer and state builder. He was a courageous soldier who fought fiercely against his enemies. He was also a diplomat and a peacemaker, who extended friendship to every native group he encountered. He may have formed these alliances for selfish reasons, but by making friends with the Indians, he gained their trust and the freedom to explore their land safely with native guides. These alliances also kept the peace and preserved the life and culture of native peoples. They proved mutually beneficial to both Europeans and native peoples.

Unfortunately, few of the men who followed in Balboa's footsteps had such values. Men such as Pedrarias Davila, Hernando Cortéz, and Francisco Pizarro saw in the New World only wealth to plunder and territory to own and exploit. They showed little concern for native peoples.

Balboa's legacy lives on in such monuments as this impressive statue in Panama City, Panama.

They turned Spanish America into an empire that had no democratic base. This heritage of Spanish control and violence was costly to the peoples who eventually won their independence in Central and South America. Few were able to incorporate the democratic ideals that succeeded in the United States and Canada into their governments. For two centuries these countries floundered in deep poverty and corruption, ruled by military strongmen and corrupt dictators.

Darién—Sad Fate of the First Settlement

Darién, one of Balboa's greatest accomplishments, did not long outlive its founder. Pedrarias wasted no time after Balboa's execution in establishing a new capital for the colony on the west coast, which he named "the great city of Panama." Most residents of Darién moved to Panama and, in 1529, Pedrarias forced those still in the settlement to leave. He took everything of value from Darién, including supplies, to Panama City. Only a few people too old or sick to travel remained behind. Before the year was out, the Indians attacked and killed those few and set the remaining buildings on fire.

The once proud capital of the first colony on the American mainland was soon reclaimed by the surrounding forest. But its name lived on for a time, becoming the name for all the territory that extended westward to the Pacific.

After Balboa's death, Pedrarias moved his base of power from Darién to the new settlement of Panama City, pictured here in 1748.

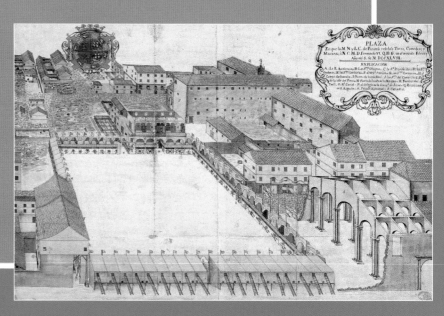

Afterword

Would it have been different if Balboa had lived? Perhaps not. He was only one man, and his very downfall showed that he was out of step with the cold bureaucrats who came to control Spanish America. But what if Balboa and not Pizarro had been the conqueror of the Inca empire of Peru? Is it possible that some of that great culture and its people might have survived?

After Balboa's death, Pedrarias did everything he could to erase any memory of the conquistador. He had his name removed from all documents pertaining to the discovery of the Pacific and other places, naming himself as the sole discoverer of the region. But the men who

The cruelty of the Spanish to the Native Americas left a harsh legacy in their New World colonies.

Balboa's Dream— The Panama Canal

In 1517 Balboa wrote in his journal of an idea for a canal between the two seas that would make the overland crossings of the isthmus he endured unnecessary. This canal remained a dream until 1881 when the French, who had already built the successful Suez Canal in Egypt, attempted it. They abandoned the work after seven years of tremendous effort. In 1904 the Americans began work on a canal. Unlike the French canal, theirs would have locks to change the level of the water as ships passed through it. After ten years of work that cost more than $366 million, the Panama Canal was completed. It officially opened in August 1914—nearly 400 years after Balboa first proposed it.

Since then, friction developed between the United States and Panama over U.S. control of the canal and the surrounding land called the Canal Zone. U.S. president Jimmy Carter signed a treaty with Panama in 1977 that gave control of 64 percent of the Canal Zone to Panama in 1979. The canal itself and the remaining land of the Canal Zone were turned over to Panama at noon on December 31, 1999. Protection of this valuable waterway is now the responsibility of Panama.

A tugboat tows an American battleship through the Panama Canal in 1915, the year after it opened. The canal connected the Atlantic and Pacific Oceans.

Despite the tragedy of his early death, Balboa is remembered today as one of the greatest early explorers of the Americas.

knew and loved Balboa kept his name and his accomplishments alive. Today Pedrarias Davila is a footnote in history while Balboa is considered one of the New World's greatest explorers. His name lives on in the Panamanian seaport that sits alongside the great Panama Canal he was the first to envision. The Panamanian currency, the balboa, is also named in his honor.

In the end, what history has left us with is a great explorer whose life inspired others to explore the unknown and to change the world.

Vasco Nuñez de Balboa and His Times

1475   Balboa is born in Jerez de los Caballeros, Spain.

1501   He sails to the Coast of Pearls in South America with Don Rodrigo de Bastidas.

1502–1510   He becomes an unsuccessful farmer on Hispaniola.

1510   He becomes a stowaway on a ship going to South America, leads an expedition to the east coast of present-day Colombia and Panama, and establishes the settlement of Darién.

1510–1513   As governor of Darién, Balboa explores the region and makes friends with native peoples.

1513   Balboa reaches the Pacific Ocean on September 29 after marching across the isthmus of Panama.

1514   Pedrarias Davila, a Spanish nobleman, arrives in Darién as the new governor.

1515   King Ferdinand makes Balboa governor of the South Sea, Panama, and Cuba.

1516–1517   Balboa builds four ships on the west coast of Panama and sails them into the Pacific.

1518   Balboa is arrested by his friend Francisco Pizarro under orders from Pedrarias.

1519 He is convicted of treason and executed in the public square of Acla.

1520 Ferdinand Magellan enters Balboa's South Sea and renames it the Pacific.

1533 Francisco Pizarro completes his conquest of the Inca empire in Peru.

Further Research

Books

Ash, Maureen. *Vasco Nuñez de Balboa*. Chicago: Childrens Press, 1991.

Crosthwaite, Luis Humberto; translated by Debbie Nathan and Willivaldo Delgadillo. *The Moon Will Forever Be a Distant Love*. El Paso, TX: Cinco Puntos Press, 1997.

Lomask, Milton. *Explorers*. New York: Atheneum, 1988.

Marcovitz, Hal. *Vasco Nuñez de Balboa and the Discovery of the South Sea*. Broomall, PA: Chelsea House Publishers, 2002.

Rivas, J.R. Martinez. *Vasco Nuñez de Balboa*. Cincinnati, OH: Aims International Books, 1996.

Web Sites

Vasco Nuñez de Balboa

http://www.win.tue.nl/engels/discovery/balboa.html

http://www.enchantedlearning.com/explorers/page/b/balboa.shtml

Hispanos Famosos

http://coloquio.com/famosos/balboa.html

Pizarro and Other Conquistadors

http://www.pbs.org/opb/conquistadors/home.html

BIBLIOGRAPHY

Anderson, Charles L. G. *Life and Letters of Vasco Nuñez de Balboa.* New York: Fleming H. Revell Company, 1946.

Garrison, Omar V. *Balboa: Conquistador, the Soul-Odyssey of Vasco Nuñez, Discoverer of the Pacific.* New York: L. Stuart, 1971.

Knoop, Faith Yingling. *A World Explorer: Vasco Nuñez Balboa.* Champaign, IL: Garrard Publishing Company, 1969.

Mirsky, Jeannette. *Balboa, Discoverer of the Pacific.* New York: HarperCollins, 1964.

Riesenberg, Felix, Jr. *Balboa: Swordsman and Conquistador.* New York: Random House, 1964.

Romoli, Kathleen. *Balboa of Darién: Discoverer of the Pacific.* Garden City, NY: Doubleday, 1953.

Sterne, Emma Gelders. *Vasco Nuñez Balboa.* New York: Random House, 1978.

Syme, Ronald. *Balboa, Finder of the Pacific.* New York: William Morrow, 1956

Source Notes

Chapter 1:

p. 9 "gold, silver, lead . . . ": Milton Lomask, *Exploration: Great Lives*, p. 14

p. 10 "Other World," "a very great continent": *World Book*, Vol. 4, p. 695.

Chapter 3:

p. 24 "put the herb on their arrows": Lomask, p.15.

Chapter 4:

p. 33 "I have learned very great secrets . . .": Lomask, p.17.

Chapter 5:

p. 41 ". . . the captain caused a fine tree to be felled . . . ": Kathleen Romoli, *Balboa of Darién: Discoverer of the Pacific*, p. 159.

Chapter 6:

p. 45 "now and for all time . . . ": Romoli, p. 163.

Chapter 7:

p. 53 ". . . I was rejoiced to read letters . . . ": Hal Marcovitz, Vasco *Nuñez de Balboa and the Discovery of the South Sea*, p. 113.

Chapter 9:

p. 65 "His declaration availed him not at all . . . ": Romoli, p. 342.

INDEX

Page numbers in **boldface** are illustrations.